THE

Indigenous

WOMAN'S

GUIDE

— TO —

SUCCESS

THE
Indigenous
WOMAN'S
GUIDE
—TO—
SUCCESS

Biblical Principles & Indigenous Wisdom to Help You
Discover Creator's Pathway
to the Abundant Life

SIERA TAKETCHERA RUSSELL

ISBN: 9798351328119

Interior Design: Amit Dey

DEDICATION

To Creator Sets Free (Jesus),
who turned my ashes into beauty.

TABLE OF CONTENTS

A GIFT FOR YOU

Huni'gum,

That's my way of saying "thank you" in the Yavapai language. I'm honored that you chose my book.

In the Yavapai tradition, please accept a gift from me.

As a tribal elder, I offer you success principles for abundant living, *The 7 Keys to Achieve Your Dreams* guide.

Go to: Gift.IndigenousMentors.com.

N'ach gavavie ngum. I will keep you in my prayers (Yavapai).

Siera Taketchera Russell

FOREWORD

For several generations now, the Indigenous Peoples of North America have had to walk in two worlds. The new world that invaded our lives has been forcing its colonial mold on us to transform us into its image. For a long time now, we have been pushed out of sight and out of mind, relics of an age gone by, silenced by an overwhelming flood, romanticized or demonized by many books and movies. It has been an arduous trail of many tears. A trail most are still walking. Like the recent fires that have devastated our forests, leaving behind scorched and marred remnants of their beauty, too many of our Native Peoples struggle to retain the beauty of our cultures.

But out of the ashes Creator has been birthing new beauty. He is turning our mourning into dancing. A new generation is finding their voice. The prayers of our ancestors have borne fruit. This land needs the wisdom that Creator has hidden deep within the first peoples he sent here. Each generation has its spirit warriors who have fought to bring healing to the next.

I believe Siera Russell is one of those spirit warriors. Creator has given her a vision for our Indigenous Peoples and in this book, specifically for our Indigenous Women. She not only has the "ability to see things as they are," but also "the vision to see things as they could be." She gives "success" new meaning from an indigenous perspective. Success in Western eyes often means winning at any cost, using the system to rise above all others. But from an indigenous perspective success means fulfilling the dream Creator has called one to and integrating that dream into our communities.

In my view, Siera Russell has the gift of taking the best from our Native wisdom and spirituality, combining that with the teachings of Creator Sets Free (Jesus) in profoundly practical ways, and then merging them with the best research found in the Western world.

I consider this book to be good medicine, not only for our Indigenous Women, but for all who long for a better world.

Terry M. Wildman
Lead Translator and Project Manager
First Nations Version New Testament

INTRODUCTION

I am here on earth for just a little while.

—Psalm 119:19 (GNT)

Remember that I am just a woman living a very abundant life. Every step I take forward is on a path paved by strong Indian women before me.

—Wilma Mankiller,
Principal Chief Cherokee Nation

*A*ho, my elder indigenous sister!

Maybe you don't think you need to read this book today, but an open door to help indigenous sisters may close for good if you don't. Indeed, you'd miss out on much love and joy if you overlooked the opportunity to comfort a broken heart.

The future of tribal nations lies in our children and the women who give them life. But due to unresolved trauma, we're losing too many children to suicide, drug abuse, and violence. We're also losing the God-given talents of our indigenous sisters drowning in grief.

Here's my challenge to you. Let's do our part to help our indigenous sisters heal from the spiritual wounds caused by violence and historical trauma.

Violence against indigenous women began when Columbus washed up on our shores in 1492. He raped and killed Indian women with reckless abandon and bragged about it in his journals. Since that invasion, the violence hasn't stopped. Soldiers also bragged in their journals about raping Indian women in the numerous forced removals, such as the Trail of Tears. [1]

During colonization, the U.S. military waged bloody massacres against women and children as a strategic means to wipe out a tribal nation. The Sand Creek massacre is an example.

Recently, the federal government detailed the history of violence against Native children in a 2022 report that described their Indian boarding schools' legacy of cultural genocide for over 150 years. Churches operated many of these schools. The children were seen as little "savages," and the goal was to "Kill the Indian, Save the Man." As a result, most Natives reject Christianity because people brutally forced the gospel on them or their relations.

One in three Native American women will be raped in her lifetime.[2]

---

[1] Wilbur, M. & Keene, A. (Hosts). (2021, May 5) Protect Indigenous Women (No. S3 E2) [Audio podcast episode]. In All My Relations Podcast. https://www.patreon.com/allmyrelationspodcast .

[2] Erdrich. L. (2013). Also the author of "The Round House." New York Times Op Ed, February 27, 2013, on page A25: Rape on the Reservation.

Thousands of indigenous women and girls go missing or murdered each year.[3]

These women are all our relations. They are our mothers, daughters, cousins, sisters, or aunties. Their absence leaves thousands more indigenous women grief-stricken and isolated.

These precious women are in our communities, on reservations, in urban and rural areas, and in our churches. They are our neighbors.

When a woman deeply grieves too long, bitterness and loneliness take root. The burden is heavier than she can bear alone. She doesn't cope well and isolates herself. She can't rise up into God's purpose for her life.

Because she follows Christ, traditionalists in her community may shun her. On the other hand, if she embraces her "Indianness" through contextual ministry, Native believers may disregard her. Or, her non-Native church may scrutinize her if she's too connected to her tribal heritage. These are some of the added challenges that exacerbate the isolation that Christian indigenous women may experience.

But, here's the good news!

There is also hope, perseverance, and celebrations in our communities.

---

[3] Urban Indian Health Institutue, 2018 Report including the Center for Disease Control and Prevention report that murder is the third-leading cause of death among American Indian and Alaska Native women and that rates of violence on reservations can be up to ten times higher than the national average. However, no research has been done on rates of such violence among American Indian and Alaska Native women and girls aged 10–24 living in urban areas despite the fact that approximately 71% of American Indian and Alaska Natives live in urban areas.

Creator's love through your story can change the trajectory of any life.

Your story is rich with hope and experience because you're not 20 years old anymore, right?

You're in a much better place.

But, if you're in a place where you feel hopeless, there is hope for you. You can place your feet on a good path. You don't need to give any more pain to a situation out of your control.

Maybe you're feeling hopeless over your daughter, sister, relative, or friend who isn't on a good road. Your story can change her life.

Some say there are four phases of life. From age 1-25, you're a child. Age 25-50, you're an early adult and establishing yourself in a career, establishing a family, or getting an education.

Then in the third phase, age 50-75, you're a mature adult and a phenomenon happens in this third phase—you start a reflective process. In the final stage, age 75-120, it's tough to change your life's trajectory.

I wrote this book for the indigenous woman in her third phase of life. You're reflecting on the things that gave you amazing strengths. You look back and bring the good stuff forward to change what's not working today.

You've survived the federal government's termination and assimilation policies. And you're experienced in walking between "two worlds."

You've also gone through different stages in life. You raised a family, your children are grown, and you might have grandchildren. Or, you might be a grandmother raising your grand kiddos.

In either situation, isolation occurs when kiddos grow up and move out.

Elder indigenous women wonder, "What's my purpose now? Maybe my time has passed? I had a vision, but it was so long ago."

Let me cheer you on! God has a message that only you can share with the world.

Reenvision your purpose and combat the despair of feeling deeply unneeded. Many dreams and hopes were stalled due to raising families, pursuing degrees, building careers, and so on.

In this reflective phase of life, you see the finish line more clearly than ever. Maybe you wonder how much energy you have left and if your health will last.

But, you're still young enough to make changes that move you forward in God's calling.

Indigenous women all around you are seeking God's vision for their lives. Women need to know you're in their corner. They need a safe person to listen to them, share their grief, laugh with them, and say a prayer.

Every day, God presents you with the opportunity to help another indigenous woman. God places a woman struggling with loneliness right before you. Sometimes this person could be you or me.

But it's easy to overlook these women if you think you're *unworthy*, *not ready*, or *not the best person* to help.

Do you struggle with these thoughts?

Are you lacking confidence?

Is fear holding you back?

Do you want to reenvision God's plan for your life?

Do you want to help other indigenous women succeed?

If you answered yes to any of these questions, I wrote this book for you.

I'm a Native American cross-cultural consultant and success coach. I answered "yes" to similar questions a few years back.

Some think that success is how well you perform in a career, what position or degree you hold, or your bank account. This is not true. Success is how well you master your life to fulfill God's call and live abundantly.

In this book, I share seven *indigenous secrets of success* based on scripture that have worked and continue to work in my life. They've worked for others and will work for you.

I organized this book in a self-study format with exercises at the end of each chapter. The exercises can be used for Bible study groups, church discussions, and training seminars.

Before God calls you home, help your indigenous sisters rise up in their sacred calling. When you help others, you'll rise too because a successful woman helps others succeed.

There's no need to delay. Let's get started!

CHAPTER 1

KNOW YOUR WORTH

You may think you chose me, but I am the one who chose you... I am telling you this so you will walk the road of love with each other.

—John 15:16-17 (FNV)

*Y*ou are the answer to your community's prayers. Prayers you don't even know other women are praying. Creator chose you to fulfill a purpose that only you can accomplish. This is a foundational indigenous success secret.

The Creator calls you chosen! The First Nations Version of scripture says,

> "But you who trust in Creator Sets Free (Jesus) are a chosen people. You are a family of chiefs who serve as holy men and women. You are a sacred nation, a people who belong to the Great Spirit alone. You are the ones who will show forth the beautiful ways of the one who called

you out of darkness and brought you into his wondrous light."

—1 Peter 2:9

Remember the Bible story about Esther from the tribe of Benjamin. A foreign king ruled her tribe, the Israelites, and their lives were in danger. But, God chose Esther to rescue her tribe from annihilation and protect their destiny. She *knew her worth* in God, and Esther acted even though she might have been killed.

Like Esther, God has *chosen you* for this time in the history of your tribe. National and tribal attention is focused on:

- federal boarding schools' dark legacy,
- violence against indigenous women and children,
- Native youth drug abuse and suicide,
- poverty and lack of resources.

Your story can heal your community.

Indigenous women in all age groups are contacting women who have more experience applying God's wisdom.

As an elder, you are uniquely positioned to come alongside women who struggle with isolation and shame. You're chosen to help them overcome deep sorrow from life's devasting issues, including years of pandemic social distancing.

This is the year of the "Boss Babes," explained Kelly Montijo Fink, a successful Apache musician in her fifties. This is when indigenous women must come alongside their sisters in leadership positions and help them achieve God's best for their lives.

You are in a life phase perfect for helping others. Know your worth and believe that you're chosen.

Creator chose you to be an indigenous, a spiritual "giant" for his kingdom purposes.[4] Your indigenous heritage brings spiritual strength to the body of believers. Do not give space in your mind for any shaming or unkind comments about your rich cultural heritage.

When your self-worth is based on God's Word, you move out of isolation into connection and confidence. You're quick to offer help to others.

Consider your tribal affiliation or identity. It's based on bloodline, language, or culture. But there's a higher bloodline and tribe that you belong to. Scripture says, "You are a sacred nation, a people who belong to the Great Spirit alone" (1 Peter 2:9 FNV).

You were not a mistake. It doesn't matter if your parents wanted you or not. The Creator planned your birth date, birth parents, and birthplace all for his purpose.[5]

Creator loves you so much that he called you before you were born!

---

[4] Of the Native Americans, Billy Graham once said, "The greatest moments of Native History may lie ahead of us if a great spiritual renewal and awakening should take place. The Native American has been a sleeping giant. He is awakening. The original Americans could become the evangelists who will help win America for Christ! Remember these forgotten people!" The Billy Graham Library, **Inside the Archive: Native American Headdress,** January 6, 2022, https://billygrahamlibrary.org/blog-archives-native-american-headdress/

[5] "Beginning with the first human being, he made all tribes and nations. He wanted people to live all over the face of the earth. He decided ahead of time when and where each tribe would live. He did this so that all people could look for him and find the trail that leads to him. Creator is not far away from any one of us. It is through him that we live, walk, and have our being" (Acts 17:26-28 FNV).

When you know your worth, you value the gift that you are to Creator's sacred family of believers. You *are a gift,* and you *have gifts.*

Creator Sets Free (Jesus) blessed you with a spiritual gift when you accepted him as your Savior. Scripture says:

> "Creator's gift of great kindness has been poured out on us in many ways, giving us different kinds of gifts. If your gift is to speak the heart and mind of the Great Spirit in a prophecy, then let trust guide your words. If your gift is helping others, then give yourself to help others. If teaching is your gift, teach well. If your gift is to speak courage and strengthen the hearts of others, then speak bravely. The one whose gift is giving should not hold back. If your gift is leading, lead with honor. And the one whose gift is showing mercy and kindness to others should do so freely, with a glad heart!"
>
> —Romans 12:6-8 FNV

Sadly, some elder indigenous women won't acknowledge their spiritual gifts. If this sounds like you, then your reluctance or false humility may be due to shaming and punishment practices of federal boarding schools and colonization.

You may not want to bring attention to yourself and be accused of pride. But it's not prideful, so don't hide your talent because someone said you were proud. When you know your worth, you're on high alert for opportunities to generously share your gifts.

Generosity is a core value of most tribal nations. So, be generous with what God's given you because "more is required from the ones who are given and trusted with more" (Luke 12:48 FNV).

Here's a story about knowing your worth and sharing your gift.

Lura Olander is a successful, elder indigenous choreographer. For the past twenty years, she has blessed tribal communities with dancing. Her dance ministry, called Soaring Eagles Ministry, might never have existed if she didn't know her worth to Creator.

Lura's Kiowa grandmother passed away before she could teach Lura about her Native heritage. Raised off the reservation and not enrolled in her tribal community, Lura felt unworthy to call herself indigenous. She didn't know if she was *Indian* enough to call herself a Christian native woman. She felt that tribally enrolled people wouldn't accept her. So when a native spiritual leader said she was enough "Indian in God's eyes," *knowing her value* changed her life's trajectory.

Here's Lura's story:

> "The night before a *Many Nations, One Voice* conference in Mesa, Arizona, spiritual leader Richard Twiss (Lakota) held a roundtable discussion. Richard shared a few stories and then said each person could ask him a personal question. Richard was Native and White like me. I asked, 'I've heard many Native people say that you must have a percentage of Indian blood to prove your indigenous lineage. What percentage of blood do I have to have to be called an Indian?'
>
> He thought for a second, then he looked me straight in the eyes, 'One drop.' Shocked, I replied, 'One drop?' 'Yes, one drop of blood and you are Native, not just to me, this is what God looks at. Because it took only one drop of his blood that was shed on the cross to cover all sins. Every

indigenous person had one drop of blood covering his or her life. So, in my opinion, that's the only amount of blood you must have. More than that, I can tell that you have plenty of love in your heart for Native people. This is what really makes you Native.'"

Richard's message freed Lura from the isolation, shame, and toxic thoughts that she wasn't *good enough*, *not enough Indian,* or *worthy* to come alongside indigenous people.

Once Lura believed that God chose her to be indigenous, not solely based on blood quantum but on her love for Native people, she rose up into her calling. Lura bloomed as a gifted choreographer of Native and Messianic worship dancing for indigenous communities.

Like Lura, act on your identity in Creator Sets Free (Jesus) and offer your God-given talent to help other indigenous sisters succeed.

Another story comes from Kelly, a gifted musician and prophetic seer I mentioned earlier. Creator told Kelly that this is the year of the "Boss Babe" and to acknowledge and support women in leadership positions. Creator also called her to lead specific areas and support other leaders.

Kelly's unique gift is in music. She recently received a nomination for a Native American Music Award in the "Best Christian Inspirational" category.

Here's Kelly's story about helping an indigenous woman succeed in her vision:

> "One Sunday afternoon, I read a newspaper article about this new store in my town. The article was about a silversmith, and she's Apache! I thought, 'What! There's

another Apache in Iowa City!' I was so excited that I looked her up on Facebook. I sent a message to her business that said, 'I found you in the papers, and I'm also Apache. I'm so glad you're here. Can I come to visit your shop and talk to you?' She was sweet and said, 'Oh yeah, come and visit.'

We soon met, and it turned out that she and her husband were also believers. Here's what's really cool about her business. Her shop is *House of Dotl'izhi* (Dot-Cluh-Gee), which means *House of Turquoise*. And the tagline is: Know Your Value, Know your Beauty, Know your Strength. She targets women customers in their forties and fifties. She compares these women to turquoise—valuable, beautiful, and strong. I also believe elder indigenous women are valuable, beautiful, and strong too!"

But Kelly's story didn't end with meeting the Apache businesswoman.

When an indigenous woman *knows her worth,* she shows up to help other women succeed.

After Kelly met with the *House of Turquoise* owner, she committed to helping her establish the business. In addition, God led Kelly to help a non-indigenous sister, a Lutheran preacher.

Like Kelly, God chose you to help your indigenous sisters overcome obstacles and achieve their dreams. You can help by mentoring, encouraging, teaching, praying, listening, and so on.

Sometimes it's hard for women to acknowledge their gifts; it's even more difficult to share them. If this sounds like you, ask Creator for the courage to approach a hurting sister and say, "These are my gifts; how can I help you?"

Please don't save your gift for a rainy day. No one can receive a gift that you never offered. Don't miss out on all the love and joy from helping another woman achieve her dreams.

Know your worth and believe that God chose you to be a "Boss Babe," too.

Take Action:

- Vocalize your gift. Pray and ask Creator for his wisdom and courage to talk about your talents or skills with trusted friends.

- Call a close friend and tell her how your life is better with her in it. Ask your friend how you've blessed her life.

- Pray and ask Creator to help you see the people in your life that need someone to walk alongside them.

- Select an indigenous woman in your community who is starting a new business or ministry. Introduce yourself and offer one to three hours of your time each week to help her succeed.

- Contact your tribal administration and offer to mentor young women in your field of knowledge or experience.

- Contact your community, church family, or spiritual group leaders and ask how you can serve for two to four hours every month. Ask if any young woman needs mentoring.

Let's move forward into Creator Sets Free's (Jesus) two great success secrets or instructions for living an abundant life:

> "Love the Great Spirit from deep within, with the strength of your arms, the thoughts of your mind, and the courage of your heart; and, love your fellow human beings in the same way you love yourself."
>
> —Matthew 22:37-39 FNV

CHAPTER 2

WALK IN LOVE

Other people are going to find healing in your wounds.
Your greatest life messages and most effective ministry
will come from your deepest hurts.

—Rick Warren, *The Purpose-Driven Life*

Two people are better off than one, for they can help each
other succeed. If one person falls, the other can reach out
and help. But someone who falls alone is in real trouble.

—Ecclesiastes 4:9-10 (NLT)

$\mathcal{G}$ood relationships keep us healthier and happier.[6] Healthy relationships have the power to heal the soul.

Sadly, one in every five Americans is lonely. Many indigenous women are lonely.

---

[6] Robert Waldinger, What Makes A Good Life on YouTube, https://www.youtube.com/watch?v=8KkKuTCFvzI&t=247s

Sometimes people think they're better off without relationships because they don't want to hurt others or dump all their personal trauma on others, so they isolate themselves. It's not okay to be too lonely. Because unrelenting loneliness is deadly.

But this isn't God's best for you.

God wants you to live unselfishly in healthy relationships.

Before colonization, indigenous societies placed great importance on the quality of relationships within their village. Every tribal member had an essential role in the community's economic, social, and spiritual well-being. Every person knew what she contributed to the village, from the old to the young. And each person was critical to the tribe's survival.

Pre-colonial indigenous mindset is different from the Euro-American mindset. Mainstream culture places great value on the nuclear family, romantic relationships, and self-love. Compare this to the indigenous mindset that places great value on community relationships.

Indigenous women and their tribes continue to struggle with isolation related to the aftermath of colonization and historical trauma. But, your faith is a beacon of hope.

One way to honor your ancestor's sacrifice is to heal from historical trauma. Trauma can infect your mind so profoundly that you walk in bitterness and unforgiveness. This isn't Creator's promising future (See Jeremiah 29:11 for Creator's plans for you).

I'm not saying you forget the traumas that have made you wise and strong. But you must stop allowing traumas, injustices, or regrets to become your identity. For example, American society once said it was good to "kill the Indian." Many Indians still walk in shame for who

God made them. The truth is that indigenous people have a colorful and spiritually powerful heritage and identity through Creator Sets Free (Jesus).

Maybe some church or unchurched people have said to you, "That happened a long time ago. Geez, why don't you get over it?"

But the early 1960s wasn't so long ago, and God's way to historical healing is relational and transformational. Healing comes through loving, healthy relationships.

God instructs you to take responsibility for loving others. Creator Sets Free (Jesus) said:

> "I am giving you a new road to walk. In the same way I have loved you, you are to love each other. This kind of love will be the sign for all people that you are walking the road with me."
>
> —John 13:34-35 FNV

Loving others isn't easy when they've broken your trust, which has long-lasting consequences.

When you're younger, other people tell you what to do. So you do what they say, thinking your life will work out. Especially when the *"expert"* comes in the name of God and tells you how to live. But then your life doesn't work out, and resentment takes root.

When you keep turning your life over to others, it is a way to avoid responsibility. And many women turn their life over to their husbands, counselors, bosses, or other authorities. They hand over their power to make choices. Then when bad things happen, they feel victimized.

Here's how love in a community helped me break free from a victim mindset.

I was in my fifties when God revealed that I resented a former pastor for my divorce and for shaming me because I was Indian and a woman.

At eighteen, I met a guy in church, and within a few weeks, we were engaged. Like most teenagers, I was immature. I also had low self-esteem and poor decision-making skills.

But before we married, I met with the pastor because I felt uneasy about getting married.

I asked him if I was too young. He said, "No, teenage couples are easily tempted to have pre-marital sex, so get married immediately."

So, I married an immature twenty-one-year-old *boy*.

Two months into our marriage, I met with the pastor again. I was desperate. My husband and I fought every day, and he hit me. I needed help.

The pastor said, "Stop arguing with him. Submit to your husband. He's the head of your family." I left his office feeling invisible, unworthy, and shamed.

Did my pastor give me good advice about marrying at eighteen and submitting to an abusive husband? *Certainly not.*

Can I blame my pastor for getting married at eighteen? Sure, and I did for years.

I thought, "There's no way I would have married if the pastor had simply given me better advice. Because I was an Indian woman, I wasn't as important to him as my 'white' fiancé/husband."

I allowed my bitterness and unforgiveness to control future decisions about churches. I blamed and distrusted *all* pastors. I refused
to connect with a church family for many years. I refused to send my
daughter to any church. I didn't want her to feel ashamed or *not good
enough.* My decision almost cost us our lives.

But I was wrong.

The truth is simple. God gives us free will. I had the freedom to
choose.

It was my choice to get married, and our marital problems were not
the pastor's fault.

I wandered away from the church for many years. My life spiraled
out of control. I struggled with drug addiction. [7]

In recovery, I was desperately lonely and needed to feel loved.

I contacted a community of Native believers. They showed love by
accepting and including me in their circle of friendship and ministry.
Their love helped me progress on a healing journey away from a victim mindset toward an abundant mindset.

Over time, I saw my responsibility in getting married. The truth about
my power to choose helped me forgive and release the resentment
that I carried. My unforgiveness was holding me back from the life
God intended.

Creator says, "Show goodwill and kindness to others, by releasing
them from the things they have done wrong. For this is what the

---

[7] Rising Above Opioid Addiction, An Indigenous Woman's Story of Childhood
Trauma, Faith & Healing, https://www.amazon.com/Rising-Above-Opioid-Addiction
-Indigenous-ebook/dp/B08KBYVQ95

Great Spirit, through the Chosen One, has done for you" (Ephesians 4:32 FNV).

Walking in harmony means you aren't blaming others, holding grudges, or living in regret.

God says, "Each of you should take a good look at your own deeds. Then you can feel honor in the good you have done without comparing yourself with others" (Galatians 6:5 FNV).

The healing journey requires good relationships and taking responsibility for your actions.

Here's an indigenous sister's story of her healing journey in a community.

An indigenous sister, Susan, attended a Sunrise Ceremony on the San Carlos Apache reservation. She is not a citizen of this community. A San Carlos woman asked her to come and help with a "coming of age" ceremony.

Susan is Chiricahua Apache and never learned her native tongue due to colonization.

She immediately accepted the invite, showed up at the ceremonial grounds, jumped into the camp, and did everything the community needed for a good ceremony.

Some elder Apache women noticed her initiative and hard work in setting up camp. They asked her, "Well, what do you want from this experience?"

Susan answered, "Well, I'd like to learn the Apache language."

The elder Apache women said, "We'll help you."

They connected with her and opened a door for this younger woman to get what she needed *that they had to give.*

The elder Apache women saw and shared their wisdom with Susan, a Chiricahua woman. The shame Susan carried for not speaking Apache began to heal as she spent time with these tribal elders. Due to colonization and boarding school policies, she wasn't taught her native tongue. Her parents didn't want her to suffer in school if English wasn't her first language. This is probably your experience also; it's my experience too.

But, Susan is healing because of the Apache elders.

The women willingly offered their gift of the Apache language and culture. The way they invited her into their circle of friendship is an excellent example of Creator Sets Free's great instruction to love others as yourself.

The elders gained a new, honoring relationship, a path out of loneliness for both Susan and the elders.

Taking responsibility to love others is a secret to success that rewards your life with healthy relationships.

Take Action:

1. Do an affirming exercise with a small group of women from your church, community, or circle of friends. Sit in a circle, facing inward. Start the circle with an opening prayer and read the love chapter in 1 Corinthians 13 from the Message Translation. Ask each person to say something loving or encouraging about the woman on her left. Continue going around the circle until it's a good time to close. Ask the women how they're feeling about hearing good things about themselves. Close the gathering with prayer. Plan another time to encourage one another.

2. Set aside some alone time with God. Pray and ask God where you need to take responsibility for your part in a bad situation and to stop blaming others for your attitudes, actions, or responses.

3. Read and meditate on Psalm 139:23-24 (NLT), "Search me, O God, and know my heart; test me and know my anxious thoughts. Point out anything in me that offends you and lead me along the path of everlasting life." Write down anything that comes to mind, and pray over them.

4. Ask God to search your heart and reveal any unresolved hurts or grudges you are holding. Everyone has blind spots, but God will shine a light on these areas if you humbly ask Him. What is the Great Spirit showing you?

The next indigenous secret of success is the power in your control to achieve God's purpose for your life. This power is self-discipline, and it will forever alter your life.

CHAPTER 3

CHOOSE TO DO IT NOW

A person without self-control is like a city with broken-down walls.

—Proverbs 25:28 (NLT)

When you are foolish, you want to conquer the world. When you are wise, you want to conquer yourself.

—John C. Maxwell, *The Self-Aware Leader*

Self-discipline is the superpower for abundant living. It's a "Do it now!" rather than a "Do it later" approach to life.

Get things done now, so you don't run out of time, like my Hopi sister.

"You're special, beautiful, and quite a leader," were Elaine Torchbearer's last words to me. She loved to be called "Torch," and she was a courageous, Hopi elder *on fire* for God. She grew up on the

Hopi reservation and dearly loved her people. Torch devoted her life to helping indigenous women succeed wherever God planted them.

She disciplined herself to faithfully call her list of Native sisters and leave an encouraging message. She continued these acts of love even though she was suffering from a painful medical condition in her final years of life.

I replay her loving voicemails whenever I need encouragement.

While bedridden, she left her last message in 2019. She expressed sadness and urgency to continue helping Native people before she died.

Torch knew that I was a tribal councilwoman. She disciplined herself to pray and regularly sent me encouraging messages, which were similar to her final one:

> "Hi. This is Elaine Torchbearer. I love you so much. I pray for you. I praise God for you. *My heart feels heavy, and I've been weeping for our people. I wish I could drive and do what He wants me to.* You're special. Let me know what's going on. So I'll know how to definitely pray for you. I lost my voice Sunday, so everyone was happy. (chuckles) Sorry but I'm getting it back. (chuckles) *The Lord bless you and give you the strength to do what you must.*"

Torch's time on earth was done.

I'm forever grateful that she did the phone call *at that moment* and didn't wait until tomorrow. Because for Torch, tomorrow didn't come.

She epitomized a successful indigenous elder who supported other women to achieve their God-given purpose. Through her disciplined actions, she demonstrated God's love.

Many indigenous women are stronger today because of Torch's life.

Live a disciplined life and influence your community for God's glory. The Bible says:

> "Walk in a good way among those who are outsiders to our spiritual ways...when they see the good you have done, they will give honor to the Great Spirit on the day he comes to visit us."
>
> —1 Peter 2:12 FNV

Disciplining yourself to finish what God asks of you is the hallmark of success.

Do *what matters* so your life serves as an example and brings glory to God.

Here's a story about reducing stress with self-discipline.

One day in graduate school, a professor assigned a substantive writing project due in two weeks. Later that evening, my Canadian classmate sat on her dorm floor with books and papers spread all over. Curious, I leaned in and asked what she was doing; she replied with a kind smile, "The writing assignment—two weeks pass quickly!"

My thinking was that the paper wasn't due for two weeks, so why do it now? So, I continued to avoid my writing assignment for the next twelve days. But as the due date approached, I became super-stressed, and I turned it in at the very last moment.

My colleague completed the project ahead of time, stress-free. Self-discipline was superior to procrastination.

Be quick to say, "I'll do it today, and do it to the best of my ability!" Then follow through.

Here are two steps to becoming more disciplined:

1. Realize it isn't the easiest path to choose.
2. Commit to it as a full-time activity, day by day.

When you apply these steps, you'll discover that each disciplined effort will ultimately reap a deep sense of joy and satisfaction.

Push through the tough times, and you'll be amazed by what God accomplishes through you.

Here's a story about self-discipline that will help focus your perspective.

During final exams, a Native student asked to speak with me privately. Sadness covered her face, and her voice shook as she told me her story.

My mom is having heart problems, and she needs me. I can't study. It's not a good time to think about law school. I'll go back to my former career.

I listened, encouraged, and offered her another perspective.

She remembered her dream to be a Native attorney for her tribe. She remembered all her sacrifices to attend law school and her community obligations.

She put her impulses aside and focused on her dream of becoming an attorney. Her mother didn't want her to quit school and supported her decision.

Self-discipline overcame her sadness, worry, and inaction. It helped her pass the final exams.

Self-discipline helped her to become an influential political leader in Indian Country.

There's a deep sense of joy and satisfaction when you have self-discipline and persevere to accomplish what God sets before you.

You must say "yes" to things you don't enjoy and say "no" to something you want every day of your life. Otherwise, taking the easy road delays or prevents reaching your potential.

Here's a story of self-discipline moving me forward.

I experienced the most devastating phone call one week after my law school graduation ceremony. The registrar said I had failed a class and didn't have enough credits to graduate. My knees buckled, and my body slumped. Fortunately, a friend was nearby.

I was angry that the registrar didn't reveal my failing grade before I went through the graduation ceremony. I had accepted a position in another state that required a Juris Doctorate.

I could have become consumed with anger and blamed everyone connected with the grading process. I could have become resentful and considered myself the victim, but this choice would have kept me from moving forward.

I sought advice from a trusted friend who had recently graduated. She shared the story of another graduate who faced a similar scenario, retook her exam, passed her class, and was a successful attorney.

I decided that if she could do it, then I could too. So, I humbled myself and met with the professor. He allowed me to retake the exam within two weeks.

In preparation for a marathon of studying, I planned out every hour —when to sleep, eat, grocery shop, prepare food, do library research, and study. I used every resource imaginable to free up my time to learn twelve weeks of material in less than two.

I had legitimate reasons for failing that class. But, I changed my focus from "poor me" to "I can pass this class. I can do it!"

I didn't *feel* like putting in the extra hard work of organizing and studying in a short time. But, I couldn't base what I needed to do on whether I actually felt like doing it. I had to focus on studying.

In two weeks, I taught myself criminal procedure. Under normal conditions, law professors teach this subject over thirteen or fourteen weeks.

I feared that I would fail again when I retook my exam. I feared losing my new position if I failed this exam. I feared what my family and daughter would think. But I had to take the exam despite my fears.

I made no excuses and persevered. Self-discipline triumphed over my fears.

I passed the exam.

Dreams become a reality when we keep our commitment to them. Discipline yourself and finish the hard things for God's glory. These daily tasks, responsibilities, and assignments shape you into a person of integrity.

Self-discipline gives you the power to accomplish your God-given purpose with excellence.

Persevere in doing the right things at the right time in your life. Your life serves as an example. Self-discipline inspires others to achieve their dreams.

Indigenous women are watching. They will seek you for coaching, mentoring, accountability, or encouragement. Be prepared.

God will help you exercise restraint over any impulses, emotions, or desires hindering you from achieving your dreams. Just ask him. Remember that you've received a spirit of power, love, and *self-discipline*, not fear or timidity (2 Timothy 1:7 NLT).

1. Set aside five minutes and think about an important goal or dream that you want to accomplish. Something you've attempted, but you haven't completed yet. Then, close your eyes and pay close attention to your feelings when you *see yourself achieving* that goal.

   In the morning, right when you wake up, recall your feelings about accomplishing that goal or dream. Think about how wonderful you will feel to have that thing, be that thing, contribute to that thing, or make that difference. Repeat this every morning so it becomes a practice.

   This practice allows you to connect your heart to the dream or goal. When your heart engages with your goals, it helps you remember the payoff, the benefit, or the significant reasons for staying on track. Passion motivates you to get it done today— not tomorrow. [8]

2. Set social rewards as a payoff when you get a small win towards achieving your goals. Celebrating any accomplishment with others reinforces your choices to make goals happen.

   For example, if you're writing a book, share a win with a friend whenever you complete a chapter. You can call her up and tell her what you've achieved, discuss the process, and receive a virtual high-five. Maybe you'd invite a friend out for a celebratory cup of coffee or beverage of her choice. You

---

[8] Brandon Burchard's message on YouTube titled "4 Ways to Become More Disciplined:"

and your brain need to celebrate the small wins to keep the benefits of discipline fun and worth repeating every day.

3. Get an accountability friend, group, or partner to keep you on target to achieve your goals.

The next *secret to success* is key to fulfilling God's purpose for your life.

CHAPTER 4

WRITE YOUR VISION

Write down clearly on tablets what I reveal to you, so that it can be read at a glance.

—Habakkuk 2:2 (GNT)

The Sacred Teachings tell us that no human being has ever seen or heard or imagined all the good things the Great Spirit has planned for the ones who love him.

—1 Corinthians 2:9 (FNV)

*G*ive yourself permission to dream again. The season may have changed, but God's vision for your life hasn't. He placed a call in your heart that is still there. No matter how much time has passed, your call is still the same.

Do you sense the Holy Spirit gently tugging at your heart but you're unsure what's next? You can find clarity in God's vision for your life. Sight is the ability to see things as they are and vision is the capacity to see things as they could be.

God wants us to clearly see his vision. God says that without vision people will die (Proverbs 29:18). Vision keeps people progressing. It takes you from where you are right now to where Creator calls.

Vision is the key to living a life of purpose because where there's a dream, there's hope. Where there's hope, there's faith to believe all things are possible with the help of the Great Spirit (Matthew 19:26 FNV). Scripture says, "Trusting Creator is the solid ground our hope rests on. It means we can be sure of the things we do not see" (Hebrews 11:1 FNV).

In Genesis, Abraham lived in the desert surrounded by sand in the day and stars at night. God told Abraham, "Look up into the sky and count the stars if you can. That's how many descendants you will have!" (Genesis 15:5 NLT). He later told Abraham to *look* at the grains of sand because they also represented the number of future descendants. God wanted Abraham *to visualize* the promised future.[9]

Every day, Abraham *saw* God's vision all around him.

Abraham trusted God, left everything familiar behind, and followed God's direction. Because of his great faith, Abraham became the father of many nations.

Keep God's vision before your eyes and see your dreams become a reality.

Anna, a prophetess, was an eighty-four years old Jewish woman when she saw her vision come true. When her husband died, she was still a young woman. But, Anna had a vision that a messiah would come one day and save her people. So Anna worshipped,

---

[9] Terri Savelle Foy, *Dream It. Pin It. Live It.*

fasted, and prayed day and night in Jerusalem's Temple. She never left. The Temple kept God's vision of Israel's redemption before her eyes every day.

As she aged, Anna probably questioned whether her vision would be fulfilled during her lifetime, but she persevered. She was focused on God's vision.

Then one incredible day, Anna saw her vision come to pass. Mary and Joseph brought baby Jesus to the Temple, and Anna thanked the Creator (Luke 2:36-38 FNV).

One lesson from Anna's story is that you're never too old, and it's never too late to see God's vision for your life come to pass.

God planted desires within your heart to bless others. But, your dreams may be buried beneath years spent raising families, building careers, or other obligations. Vision opens your faith eyes to your God-given dreams.

Let's envision what God planted in your heart long ago.

In 2014, while in my late fifties, I enrolled in an online course called "Make This Your Best Year Ever." I learned about vision boards as a tool to focus on where I wanted to go. Every year since that class, I have created vision boards. Writing my vision down has kept me moving forward in God's calling.

Here's when I reenvisioned God's purpose for my life.

I was a law professor teaching Criminal Procedure, International Human Rights Law, and Federal Indian Law. I ended my professorship when my dad asked me to return home and help with his health concerns.

It was tough to leave my faculty position because I loved working with students. But, I took leave and left for the reservation.

My dad was a respected tribal leader serving his community for over forty years. He had a lifetime vision of economic prosperity for our tribal nation.

After my dad passed, I followed in his footsteps and served in tribal politics. Fortunately, my community elected me to serve on the council for three years. When my term ended, I stood figuratively at a cliff's edge. I didn't know God's plan for me.

I questioned whether I should run for reelection. Reelection meant doing legislative work for another three years. That didn't seem to be a good fit for the long term. If I didn't get reelected, what would I do?

I felt stuck.

I prayed and asked:

- What can I do with my thirty-plus years of career experience and education?
- What is God's vision for my life?
- Am I still passionate about the same things from my twenties or fifties?
- What do I see myself doing in the next few years?

Then I attended the *Lifestyle Freedom Event* in Costa Rica hosted by Donna Partow, best-selling Christian author, and Tamara Aragon, business marketing consultant. It was an intense, 7-day training that included seeking God's vision, business coaching, one-to-one consultations, teaching, mastermind groups, and self-paced instruction.

Five days into our program, I had my "aha" moment! God formed a picture in my mind's eye while talking to another attendee. I envisioned connecting indigenous women around the world so they could help each other fulfill their destinies. I reenvisioned my childhood dream to teach Native children. I immediately wrote my vision down, and I shared it with my colleagues.

When I returned home, I placed my vision where I could see it every day. I set goals to turn my dream into a reality.

Eventually, I published my first book and founded Indigenous Mentors, which provides coaching, training, and mentoring for indigenous women seeking to expand their influence and impact.

My journey proves that it's never too late to reenvision your future. You will get God's vision for your life when you're ready to receive it.

You don't need to travel to a faraway land or attend a week-long event.

But, you must make quality, focused time alone with God, eliminate distractions, and seek his will for you.

Accessing your God-given vision requires gratitude, prayer, humility, focus, expectancy, and persistence.

God says, "I know the plans I have for you... plans to prosper you and not to harm you, plans to give you hope and a future" (Jeremiah 29:11).

Apostle Paul wrote, "My one aim is to forget what is behind me and keep moving forward, dancing the victory dance with firm steps *to the drumbeat of Creator's heart* (Philippians 3:13 FNV). Like Paul, you must keep moving forward in Creator's vision for you. However, you can't move forward unless you can see your destination.

Notice that the root word of destination is "destiny." God's vision gives you your destiny.

God instructed Habakkuk to write his vision to clarify it (Habakkuk 2:2 GNT). So, write your vision down using words, pictures, or images. I highly recommend making a vision board.

Vision boards are tools to focus you on God's purpose and remember the dreams he's placed in your heart. God designed our brains to think in pictures and images. Abraham had the stars at night and the sand in the day to remind him of his destiny.

Vision boards aren't magical. They are simply a visible display of the images that come to mind representing God-given desires in your heart.

When you clearly see your vision, you are on track to making your dreams a reality.

When you feel insecure or stuck, seek God's point of view on your future. Vision is not your private view of the future; instead, it's a view of your God-inspired future.

Imagine God's best for you. Then, write your vision down. It is a *secret to success* that keeps you focused and on track.

Take Action:

≪——◇——≫

1. Storytelling is a way tribal elders pass on cultural knowledge and wisdom. If you feel more comfortable sharing your vision through a story, record yourself talking about your dreams.

2. Make time to imagine God's best. Sit down with a piece of paper and a pencil. Ask the Holy Spirit to reveal Creator's vision for your life. Write down what you envision. If it's not too painful, think about when you were a child. When you were a little girl, what was your dream? Write down what has always been in your heart. Don't be afraid to write it on paper. Write it down and make it clear.

3. Write down what comes into your mind when you read the following questions:

   - Place your hand over your heart. What dream have you locked away?

   - What would you want to achieve if you had only one year to live?

   - What do you hope people will say about you at your funeral?

   - What would you do if you knew you couldn't fail?

   - How would you spend your last twenty-four hours?

4. Make a vision board. It's more than a fun dream-building project; it's framing your future! You can find vision board-making videos on YouTube. Search for *how to make a vision board*. The materials you need:

- One poster board, a corkboard (plus push pins), or a magnetic board (with magnets).

- A collection of pictures (magazines, postcards, newspaper clippings, brochures, online images, etc.) that you don't mind cutting into pieces. The more VARIETY, the better!

- Personal photos: using personal photos on the board lets you clearly see yourself living that dream. Use your personal photographs to pin or paste next to your goal.

- Any scrapbooking supplies and motivational phrases.

- Glue, scissors, tape, glitter, stickers, and stamps.

5. Consider having a vision board party with a few trusted friends. Pray over each board and encourage each other. Set goals for accomplishing your dreams.

Congratulations on giving yourself permission to dream because vision clarifies God's direction. The following *success secret* is the fuel for your dreams.

CHAPTER 5

RELEASE YOUR POTENTIAL

To reach your potential you must grow. And to grow,
you must be highly intentional about it.

—John C. Maxwell, *Success Is a Choice*

*A*s elder indigenous women, we've had roles assigned to us throughout our lives, and we've been afraid to take the position God has given us. God's not done with you. His plan for your life goes beyond what you've already accomplished.

Picture an oak tree growing near a river. See its towering height with massive leafy branches. Imagine planting a seed from that oak tree in a two-foot container. The seed will not grow into the magnificent oak tree because the container isn't big enough for its potential.

God planted a seed of greatness in you (Genesis 1:26-28). You are a vessel for untapped potential, which only you can release.

Whether you're a grandmother, former tribal leader, or retiree, you have hidden potential for significant achievements.

Potential is not what you have done already; it's what you could do but haven't done yet. When you release your potential, it sets off a chain reaction, a burning desire, in the heart of other women to also pursue their God-given destiny. Your example inspires women to push beyond the status quo and release their potential to achieve God's best in their lives.

How do you release your potential?

You release it by boldly stepping out of your comfort zone and doing what's only possible with God. The phrase *comfort zone* refers to a sense of ease and comfortability. When you picture your comfort zone, you may think of your favorite chair with a soft blanket or hanging out with close friends. But God calls you out of your comfort zone.

Pastor Francis Chen says that God doesn't call you to be comfortable. Instead, God calls you to trust him so completely that you're unafraid to put yourself in situations where you will be in trouble if God doesn't come through. It's exercising your faith muscles and doing what God requires—that you haven't done yet.

You release your potential when you follow God's leading into new areas of discipleship, mentoring, teaching, exhorting, encouraging, and serving others. You must take risks.

Here's a story showing a picture of potential when it's released. Maria, a politically connected and successful intertribal executive, shared:

> "Early in my position, I attended an all-day meeting in Window Rock on the Diné (Navajo) Reservation. I had to get back to Phoenix for another session in the morning. But, snow fell like sifted flour and blanketed the roads in Window Rock more than anyone expected.

I felt apprehensive about driving on unfamiliar roads in a snowstorm. I didn't want to get in my car and leave.

But, I remembered my father's words when I was growing up. He said, 'Whenever you are stuck and don't know the way, look for a good path left by those in front of you. Follow the tracks ahead of you through a storm because they show you that someone has been there and made it through. If they can make it through, then know that you can make it through.'

Driving through the intense and unexpected snow, I clung to his words the same way I hung onto the steering wheel! Made it to the highway and all the way home no problem."

In her story, Maria's ability to drive home safely was her potential. Although she had the potential to go the distance, she was in unfamiliar territory and apprehensive about going in the snow.

She did two things to release her potential: (1) she acted courageously, and (2) she followed a path leading her in the right direction.

To release your potential, bravely step out of your comfort zone and follow where God is calling you.

No one else has your potential; no one else has your calling. And women in your community are waiting to follow your tracks. Your light will show them the way.

Do you remember the children's song, "This Little Light of Mine?"[10] Here is a condensed version:

---

[10] Public domain.

This little light of mine, I'm gonna let it shine.

All around the neighborhood, I'm gonna let it shine.

Hide it under a bushel? No! I'm gonna let it shine.

Let it shine, all the time, let it shine. Oh yeah!

God is the light in our lives. And it's up to you to let Creator's light shine through you so you can be a light to others.

Imagine a lightbulb sitting in a box. It doesn't shine brightly; it doesn't shine at all. The lightbulb won't shine because its potential isn't being tapped into. But when you connect it to a power source, it can light up the whole room. Life works the same way. Without a power source, you can't fulfill your potential.

God is your power source. For your light to shine, you must stay connected to God. Your connection fuels your desire to love others and help them succeed.

Creator Sets Free says, "In the same way, let your light shine by doing what is good and right. When others see, they will give honor to your Father – the One Above Us All" (Matthew 5:16 FNV).

God is omnipotent. The word *Omni* means "all," and the word *potent* means "powerful ability" or "hidden energy." Omnipotent means that God is all-powerful and all-potential. Because you are created in Creator's image, you possess the potential to accomplish his purposes.

You are limited only by your imagination and limiting beliefs.

Unleashing your God-given potential is abundant living.

Don't think you're finished or have done enough because of the last big success in your life. Be careful because past success can deter you from moving forward.

Here's my version of an untapped potential story that you can find in some success books.[11] In the Swiss Alps, a famous mountain-climbing resort caters to businesses' team-building excursions. The teams start early in the morning from the resort's base camp to reach the pinnacle that day. A guide leads the teams up the cold, snow-covered mountain trail to their destination.

Halfway up the mountain, there's an Alpine lodge where the teams stop for lunch, grab hot drinks, warm up by the fireplace, and celebrate their climbing accomplishment. Then, after a short break, the guide announces it's time to gear up and head to the mountaintop. One guide describes what inevitably happens with every team.

> "Only one or two team members choose to continue the climb to the top. The rest of the team members stay behind in the lodge, enjoying the camaraderie and relaxing by the fireplace. It's as if they completely forget their goal to reach the top. They get too comfortable at the halfway point. Eventually, the shadows fall across the mountainside. The members move to the windows. They remain looking up toward the pinnacle, watching for their teammates to return. A quietness falls over the lodge as each person realizes that they'll never get another opportunity like this one they let pass by."

[11] John Maxwell, *Success is a Choice*; Joel Osteen, *Your Best Life Now*; and Terri Savelle Foy, *Dream It. Pin It. Live It.*

The reality hits that they probably will never travel to that country again and climb that mountain peak. The mountain's halfway point was not the destination. They didn't release their full potential, and they'll never know the thrill of reaching the top.

Too many people go through life using only a tiny portion of their potential. Don't let this be you!

When you were born, you entered the world bursting with potential. God blessed you with gifts, talents, and abilities. Don't stop at your last accomplishment. Don't retire your potential because "retirement" tarnishes the treasure inside. Don't be too impressed with what you've done before because there's still more unrealized potential inside you.

Here's what scripture says about the unreleased potential from the First Nations Version of the New Testament. It's called the Story of the Trusted Tribal Members (Matthew 25:14-30 FNV). It describes a tribal headman as giving three trusted tribal members a share of his goods. One tribal member received five herds of horses, one received two herds of horses, and the last received just one herd. He gave them the number of horses he knew matched their ability (*potential*) to make a good trade.

After a long journey, the tribal headman returned to see what the trusted tribal members had done with the goods he gave them.

The tribal member who received five herds went to work immediately, traded well, and earned five more herds.

> "The tribal member with two herds did the same and gained two more herds for the tribal headman. The headman was pleased with these two tribal members and honored them with more goods and all his family had.

However, the tribal member with only one herd was afraid to lose the herd, so he hid them; he had just the one herd to return to the tribal headman. The headman was very disappointed that the tribal member had played it safe and had nothing to show. The tribal headman said:

'You have *broken the trust I gave you* and have proven you are lazy and no good. The ones who do well will be given more. The ones who do nothing with it will lose even what they've been given.'"

—Matthew 25:26 FNV

The takeaway is that Creator has given you good things, gifts and abilities, to use for his Kingdom plan. Your life is valuable with a unique purpose. Please don't hide your talents and miss opportunities to bless your community.

Like Maria, who faced a sudden snowstorm, act courageously to step out of your comfort zone. Release your potential and move forward in Creator's calling. Take a leap of faith and trust Creator to work in and through you.

The Bible describes Creator as "The Maker of Life, who, by his great power working in us, can do far more than what we ask for, more than our small minds can imagine" (Ephesians 3:20 FNV).

Whatever God calls you to accomplish, he gives you the *potential* to achieve. "See! There is nothing too hard for the Great Spirit" (Luke 1:37 FNV).

Take Action:

I have had four types of people who have helped me *release my potential.* I recommend you also have these key people:

1. Cheerleader: *who is the cheerleader in your life?*

    We need an upbeat, encouraging person who will celebrate our successes. They cheer for us even when we fall short. This person thinks it's wonderful that you showed up and gave whatever you're doing a wholehearted attempt.

    If you can't think of someone, pray and ask God to help you become a cheerleader in someone else's life.

2. Accountability Partner: *who can you find to serve as your accountability partner?*

    As you clarify your dreams and goals, it's critical to your success to have someone who is also making goals happen so you can encourage each other. For example, working with an exercise partner to help you get fit or a business partner to challenge you to the next level increases successful outcomes. The key is updating one another on a routine basis: daily is ideal, but at least weekly, depending on your schedule and commitment.

3. Mentor: *who can you ask to mentor you?*

    This person already operates above the level of success you desire, whether that success is spiritual, relational, financial, or personal. Your local church or business networking meeting is an excellent place to look for a mentor because you regularly see successful people at these events. A mentor should be someone you can routinely meet face-to-face.

4. An Indigenous Coach: *who can you hire to coach you?*

   This person is a paid professional who can bring an objective perspective, create a roadmap for success, and empower you to *release your potential* to achieve your goals. A non-indigenous coach may not understand how your heritage impacts professional and personal decision-making.

An indigenous female coach is more likely to relate to your indigeneity. She has a perspective that mainstream success coaches or books can't offer. An indigenous coach knows how it feels to wonder if you're Native enough, too Native, or not enough of something connected to your ethnicity. She is better equipped to help you navigate culturally-related struggles impacting your professional and personal goals.

CHAPTER 6

CULTIVATE GRATITUDE

Always be thankful in all circumstances, for this is God's will for you.

—1 Thessalonians 5:18 (NLT)

Gratitude is the key that opens all doors, unlocks the fullness of life, abundance, prosperity, and fulfillment.

—Robert A. Emmons, *The Little Book of Gratitude*

*D*o you ever act like you have good things because you earned them? When your life is going well, it's easy to forget that everything you have is a gift from God. Pride can blind you. It can lead you to believe that your health or success is due to your own efforts.

All you have and all you are come from the Great Spirit. His will for your life is that you're always thankful (1 Thessalonians 5:18).

Think about a time when you failed to acknowledge Creator's hand in your successes. What would it look like if you thanked Creator for every moment you have?

In Chronicles 32, King Hezekiah forgot to thank God. Hezekiah was deathly ill and prayed for God's help. God miraculously healed him. But Hezekiah did not respond with thankfulness. God was angry. God knew that Hezekiah and the people of Israel could only flourish if they remembered God and practiced gratitude and humility. Fearing God's wrath, they humbled themselves and repented of pride. So the Lord's anger didn't fall on them during Hezekiah's lifetime. God mightily blessed them (2 Chronicles 32:24-32).

People who don't cultivate gratitude become independent and self-reliant. These are the pitfalls of pride that lead to destruction. A grateful heart protects against pride.

Cultivating gratitude is a constant mindset of thankfulness. It is an attitude of gratitude that becomes a lifestyle.

Over 400 Bible passages mention thankfulness. God wants gratitude to motivate everything you think, say, and do. Always express appreciation for the good in your life.

Use your words and actions to thank God and others. Without words of appreciation, gratitude falls short. The less you express thankfulness, the more arrogant you may become.

For example, God's chosen people, the Israelites, were heading to the Promised Land, but they roamed in the wilderness for over forty years. It should have been an eleven-day journey (Joshua 5:6). Instead, they complained, griped, and murmured, which caused their long wandering in the desert (Numbers 14:11-24). It was an enormous waste of time but a powerful life lesson. They didn't express gratitude to God for his miraculous blessings. They weren't thankful to their leaders. The Israelites' ingratitude wasted time, potential, and destinies. Their generation never entered the Promised Land.

Don't lose your promised land by focusing on what you don't have; instead, focus on the good you do have. Remember that God blesses grateful hearts.

God blesses your gratitude so you can bless others (Proverbs 11:25 MSG). If you follow God's instructions for life, he says that he will bless everything you do (Deuteronomy 28:1-8).

Creator blesses with good things such as love, kindness, prosperity, laughter, joy, peace, and humility. Scripture says God will achieve infinitely more than your most extraordinary request, your most unbelievable dream, and exceed your wildest imagination (Ephesians 3:20 TPT).

Love Creator with all your mind, body, and strength by showing affectionate reverence, quick obedience, and gratitude. "Give thanks to the Great Spirit in all things, for this is what he wants from you as you dance in step with Creator Sets Free (Jesus) the Chosen One" (1 Thessalonians 5:18 FNV).

Apostle Paul says, "My heart spills over with thanks to God for the way he continually empowers me, and to our Lord Jesus, the Anointed One, who found me trustworthy and authorized me to be his partner in this ministry" (1 Timothy 1:2 TPT).

Practicing gratitude means acknowledging God and the people who bless your life. A grateful heart is mindful and appreciative of ordinary things such as a cup of coffee or tea, heat in the winter, a fixed flat tire, clothes in the closet, fresh air to breathe, and so on. Gratitude prevents you from taking God and others for granted.

Don't miss opportunities to publicly thank God. Our church holds a prayer group that meets once a week called the "Assembly of Believers." The pastor begins our meeting by asking, "So who has a praise report?" or "What is God showing you?" Each person has the opportunity to give a shout-out to God!

Once I shared a praise report about something unusual that happened during a neighborhood stroll. My foot abruptly slipped off a curb's edge. I felt a twinge, but I didn't fall or twist my ankle. I immediately thanked God for protecting me. And I thanked him for my workouts with a trainer. God's provision helped prevent severe injury.

As I told my story, everyone in the group nodded in agreement. Publicly thanking God is contagious. It encourages others to reflect on God's goodness in their lives. Likewise, my relationship with God deepens when I hear others praise the Lord.

Scientific research and scripture both confirm that gratitude brings many benefits. Dr. Robert Emmons discussed the benefits of gratitude in his book, *The Little Book of Gratitude*. He writes that people who wrote down things they are grateful for had higher levels of well-being. "Writing a letter of gratitude reduced feelings of hopelessness in 88 percent of suicidal inpatients and increased their levels of optimism by 94 percent."

A brief search of the internet will tell you that scientists recognize that gratitude:

- Improves brain function and physical health
- Fosters happiness
- Improves sleep
- Strengthens and heals relationships
- Opens doors to people and opportunities

Cultivate a grateful heart by expressing gratitude for everything and everyone in your life (Psalm 100:4 AMPC).

Pastor Rick Warren mentioned three habits or ways to express gratitude to God in his sermon on "How God Blesses Grateful Hearts." These are God's love languages:

1. *Sing back to God.* God loves you and wants to hear you sing songs back to him (Ephesians 5:18-19).

   This habit of gratitude arises from scriptures that say God sings love songs about you. "The Lord, your God, is with you ... He will sing and be joyful over you" (Zephaniah 3:17 GNT).

   It's comforting to hear a mother sing a lullaby to a newborn baby. The soft, loving melody soothes and brings joy to the hearer. Similarly, when you sing your thankfulness, you bring joy to your heavenly Father (Colossians 3:16).

2. *Give back to God.* Show gratitude to God for yesterday, today, and the future (Proverbs 3:9-10).

   This habit of gratitude is tithing. To tithe is to give back to God a tenth of what God has given you. It is the first ten percent of your resources, e.g., 10 percent of your earnings before taxes. Giving back to God isn't only an act of giving it is also an act of faith. God always honors faith.

3. *Take Communion.* Partake in the Lord's Supper, the Thanksgiving Cup, and be deeply grateful for God's great gift on Calvary. When you take the body and blood of Christ, you remind yourself of whose you are and what he did for you (1 Corinthians 11:23-26).

Don't limit communion to church schedules. Expand the number of times you take the thanksgiving cup. Take communion in your home or anywhere you need his healing power.

Always be thankful.

Everything you have in life is a gift of God's love.

Take Action:

1. Pray: Dear Lord, I confess I fall into thinking that I'm fine on my own. But I'm wrong. Please give me a humble, grateful heart. I pray this in the name of Jesus.

2. Take time to think about the good things you have and the good things you have done. Acknowledge God's hand in those things.

3. Start a habit of daily thanking God. Throughout the day, pause whatever you are doing and thank God specifically for something that is making your life better.

4. Keep a gratitude journal. Each day, record five things you are thankful for and record five people who you thanked. Make this a part of your bedtime routine.

5. For the next two weeks, catch yourself complaining or griping and replace it with an expression of gratitude.

6. Write a 250-word appreciation letter to a relative, supervisor, employee, pastor, teacher, colleague, tribal council member, community leader, and so on who has impacted your life. Tell them you want to share something meaningful and ask if you can meet. Then read your letter in person and watch how your gratitude touches their heart. If it's impossible to meet face to face, drop your note in the mail. Sending a letter of appreciation via the U.S. Postal Service is an uncommon act of kindness. It brings joy to the person receiving it.

Now you're ready for the most powerful success secret. Not knowing this secret can derail the progress you've intentionally made with chapters one through six.

CHAPTER 7

PROTECT YOUR DESTINY FROM LIMITING BELIEFS

Be careful how you think; your life is shaped by your thoughts.

—Proverbs 4:23 (GNT)

The secret of our success is that we never, never give up.

—Chief Wilma Mankiller

*A*ʼho my sister.

By this point in my book, you know my definition of success. Success is becoming the woman God created you to be. God chose you and loves you regardless of what you do or don't do.

I've offered you six indigenous success secrets to help you succeed in your Kingdom purpose. The sad reality is that not everyone succeeds.

You may stop yourself.

So, here's the most crucial success secret: protect your destiny from limiting beliefs.

Limiting beliefs are the stories you repeatedly tell yourself that *hold you back* from acting or trying new things. You don't finish what you start, and you don't release your potential. You don't step out of your comfort zone. You tell yourself that you don't measure up in some area.

You base these beliefs on what you've experienced, what others have told you, or even what you've said to yourself. They can make you feel unworthy or not deserving of success.

Limiting beliefs and self-doubt sound like:

> *I'm not good enough*
>
> *What if I fail*
>
> *I don't have time*
>
> *I'm not ready because I need to fix ___*
>
> *It's too late*

Every person has doubts. So, you can't eliminate all your doubts. But you can stop rehashing them.

And, stop doubting yourself. Because God doesn't do great things for you because you're great. God does great things because he's great.

Start "doubting" your doubts. Challenge your doubts by not believing every thought that comes into your mind. Be mindful that doubts come from three sources: your old nature, Satan, and world values.

Trusting God protects against limiting beliefs. The more experience you have with God, the stronger your faith becomes.

God wants you to have deep faith. God wants you to ask and believe him for things your mind cannot fathom.

When a limiting belief comes from a deep need to control, it can manifest as overthinking or perfectionism. These behaviors are familiar to people who've experienced an unstable early life.

For example, were you raised in a home where people were drunk, fighting, and out of control? Were you raised where people were broke and couldn't get a job? Unstable home scenarios cause chaos in your soul (mind, will, and emotions). To get out of chaos, you try to control everything so it won't happen anymore. But, only God can bring lasting peace and restore souls (Psalm 23:3 NKJV).

Many people who struggle with overthinking (thinking too much about something) are unaware that it threatens success. They believe that it's prudent to give something *enough* thought. But, when it becomes procrastination, it's a threat.

Perfectionism also leads to procrastination. It is extremely stressful because you're constantly worrying about making everything perfect. Nothing is ever good enough, and the mindset robs you of feeling satisfied and fulfilled. You fret over any small decision and fail to move forward. You repeatedly ask, "How do I make this better?"

God wants you to take your thoughts captive and gain control over what you think about yourself and life (2 Corinthians 10:5 FNV). God's Word says that as a man thinks in his heart, so he is (Proverbs 23:7 NKJV).

Your thoughts and responses are completely in your control.

Your beliefs direct the decisions you make. Your decisions determine where you're headed. You'll go to exciting places or unfulfilling places, or sadly, you'll go backward.

If you believe you don't deserve abundant living, you won't make good choices for a rewarding life. God's Word says, "Be careful how you think; your life is shaped by your thoughts" (Proverbs 4:23 GNT).

False beliefs are threats to your destiny because they oppose God's Word. For example, the limiting belief: *I'm not good enough* contradicts scripture that states Christ gives you the strength to accomplish all things.

> "I have learned the secret of walking the road of life. Whether I am well-fed or hungry, whether I have more than I need or *not enough,* I can do all things through the Chosen One who gives me strength."
>
> —Philippians 4:12-13 FNV (*emphasis added*)

Several scriptures say, "Nothing is impossible with God" (Matthew 19:26; Genesis 18:14; Mark 14:36).

If you want an abundant life, take risks and make good choices. If you're satisfied with the status quo, then there isn't the opportunity for God's mighty works through you.

In scripture, Creator Sets Free (Jesus) couldn't do the mighty works he planned with the Nazarene people at the Temple because of their great unbelief (Mark:1-6 FNV). Compare this to the time when Jesus did a mighty work for the centurion's servant because of the centurion's astounding belief (Matthew 8:10).

In Judges 6, God called Gideon to lead his people into a battle that Gideon believed he *wasn't good enough* to fight. He told God there were more significant, stronger, and wiser people for this dangerous assignment. But, God had a plan that only Gideon could fulfill. When Gideon trusted the Lord, God did a mighty work through him. Gideon led his people to victory.

I've worked with indigenous women of different ages, professional backgrounds, and life goals. Unfortunately, some didn't achieve their dream due to limiting beliefs from past success.

After committing resources and time, they abandoned their plans when the journey *became too difficult*. They used a past success to justify a present failure by saying:

I've already had success doing *X*. So, I can give up on this dream because:

- It's too hard.
- I need a sign from God.
- Someone's against me.
- My family or tribe needs me more.

Here's a story about a limiting belief that could've derailed my future:

During a successful career in legal and community education, I became disabled. For seven years, I lived on social security disability. Living on disability gave me time to entertain doubts about my worth. My disability became my identity.

As I recovered, I wanted to work again. But, I didn't believe I was a desirable candidate due to years of unemployment.

My limiting belief was, "*I'm not good enough*" to apply for positions in my field. So, I only applied to minimum wage jobs.

I also wasn't applying faith and acting like God had an abundant future for me.

I had blind spots due to my limiting belief. When I confided in my mentor, Ruth Ann, she gave me a new perspective. She challenged my perception and helped me recognize errors in my thinking.

She said that I had a unique skill set and there were unique positions to match. Ruth Ann's encouragement boosted my faith in God's plan for my life. I took her advice and pursued jobs in my field.

Eventually, God opened doors to serve tribal and non-tribal communities in positions of increased responsibility, decision-making, and influence.

My self-imposed limitation could have kept me from *releasing my potential* and helping my community in significant ways.

Do you have limiting beliefs and behavior patterns that are threatening your destiny?

Here's the great news! Faith and God's Word overcome limiting beliefs *if you act.*

> "Fix your thoughts on what is true, and honorable, and right, and pure, and lovely, and admirable. Think about things that are excellent and worthy of praise."
>
> —Philippians 4:8 NLT

Overcoming limiting beliefs to fulfill God's purpose isn't easy. But it's a critical secret to success.

Sometimes, you struggle to rise above obstacles to your success, but you're never alone. The Great Spirit said, "I will never leave you or give up on you" (Hebrews 13:5 FNV).

Take control over your thoughts, let Creator give you a new way of thinking (Romans 12:2 FNV) and protect your destiny.

When your time on earth is done, you'll hear the Savior say, "well done my good and faithful servant!" (Matthew 25:23). This will be the ultimate reward.

Take Action:

1. Overcome limiting beliefs by identifying them. What are the wrong beliefs that keep you stuck? Are your thoughts building confidence or holding you back?

2. Write down all the limiting beliefs you identified that keep you from achieving your goals.

3. Challenge each belief by asking, "Is this true? What do I really believe? Where did this belief come from? Do I believe that God is going to leave me stranded or that he'll come through?" By questioning the belief, you open the possibility of changing your thinking.

4. Replace each limiting belief with a belief from scripture or personal experience that supports you. Focus on knowing your worth to God.

5. In a group: lead a talking circle for women who struggle with limiting beliefs:

   • Provide a talking stick or feather

   • Set the rules:

       ○ only the person holding the stick or feather can speak,

       ○ no one can come against others,

       ○ what is shared in the group is strictly kept in the group,

       ○ correction or direction only comes from the leader,

       ○ the circle opens with a prayer and closes with a prayer,

       ○ only the leader offers the prayers.

6. Is there something God placed in your heart that you were passionate about when you started it, but it's unfinished? Spend some time alone with God, ask forgiveness, and seek his wisdom to finish what you started.

The next chapter highlights the indigenous insider secrets of success covered in this book, plus it includes a bonus secret for living an abundant life.

CHAPTER 8

CONCLUSION

You are designed for accomplishment, engineered for success, and endowed with the seeds of greatness.

—Zig Ziglar, Motivational Speaker & Author

*C*ongratulations on reading this book and diving into the seven indigenous secrets to success.

Here's a recap:

Know Your Worth: God chose you to share a unique message with the world. Your identity is in God's Word. God calls you names that describe how special you are to Him. God gave you a purpose while on this planet. Your assignment has eternal value. If you believe God calls you chosen, you will fulfill God's purposes for your life.

Walk in Love: Accept responsibility for your attitudes and responses to situations and others' actions. You control your thoughts and behavior. Making excuses or blaming anyone or anything for your failures promotes a victim mentality and prevents progress. Love God with all your strength, mind, and actions by choosing wise and loving responses.

Choose To Do it Now: Do what matters *now*, even though it's uncomfortable. Abundant living grows from your daily choices. God is pleased with those who are quick to obey. Discipline develops the godly character that proves you can steward God's gifts well.

Write Your Vision: Sight is the ability to see things as they are. Vision is the capacity to see things as they could be. God's vision gives purpose to your life. You won't leave where you are until you can see where you'd rather be. God told the prophet Habakkuk to write his vision on tablets and make it clear. Successful people write their vision down and refer to it every day. A vision board is an excellent tool for capturing your vision and prioritizing your goals. It is a collage of images and pictures that frame your future.

Release Your Potential: Creator calls you to achieve the dreams he placed in your heart. He created you with untapped potential. Release your potential by stepping out of your comfort zone. The Creator is your biggest cheerleader. Whatever seems impossible to you isn't impossible to the Great Spirit! Creator wants you to trust him and move forward in your purpose.

Cultivate Gratitude: God wants gratitude to be the primary motivation for everything you think, say, or do. Gratitude strengthens your dependency on God and your interdependence with others. Creator desires that you are thankful all the time, no matter what situation you're facing. Practicing gratitude every day also develops a humble and generous heart. Gratitude, humility, and generosity are pillars of a successful life.

Protect Your Destiny from Limiting Beliefs: Be alert to protect your God-given purpose. Negative self-talk, fears, and limiting beliefs can keep you from achieving your potential. When your thinking doesn't align with God's word, destructive behaviors such as overthinking, perfectionism, and procrastination result. Mindfulness, faith, and God's Word are your spiritual weapons against limiting beliefs.

Bonus Secret to Success: Apply the success secrets in chapters one through seven and **take action**. Be intentional. Take your God-given message to the world.

Indigenous women are waiting for your message to help them achieve Creator's plan for their lives. Give yourself permission to pursue the dreams God put in your heart. Step out in faith.

The Bible says, "Without faith, it is impossible to please God, because anyone who comes to him must believe that he exists and that he rewards those who earnestly seek him" (Hebrews 11:6).

Your time is *now*. Go!

YOUR NEXT STEPS

A coach will help you clarify your vision and goals...keep
you focused, confront your unconscious behaviors and old
patterns...and keep you focused on your core genius.

— Jack Canfield, *The Success Principles*

*N*ow that you've read my book, you are poised to leap forward in your life and career. It's not surprising to God that you're at this pivotal point in life.

Are you seeking God's vision for your next step?

Are you ready to change the trajectory of your life?

Do you want to get a fresh, new start in any area of your life?

Imagine abundant living as you take your God-given message to the world.

To move forward, I recommend these three steps:

First:

I strongly recommend investing in yourself and hiring an indigenous success coach as your next step. Unless coached, people never reach their maximum potential.

Success coaching is a robust process that helps you get clarity and design a lifestyle, business, or career you love.

I've hired writing, business, executive, life, and success coaches to help release my potential. The coaching experience has rapidly elevated me in every area of my life: professionally, spiritually, and personally.

I'm offering to coach a limited number of women clients. Coaching provides a wide range of practical steps to get you from where you are to where you'd rather be.

I'll create a culturally relevant success coaching program tailored to your goals. For coaching, personal development, or speaking engagements, contact me at taketchera@gmail.com.

Second:

For weekly encouragement, visit www.IndigenousMentors.com and grab your free copy of the *7 Keys to Achieve Your Dreams* success principles guide. It's an easy-to-read resource for abundant living.

Third:

Join our Facebook community, Indigenous Women Leaders, where I offer mentoring tips and inspiration to encourage you in Kingdom purpose. It's a vibrant group of indigenous women of faith and their friends who make a difference in their communities.

Join here: https://www.facebook.com/groups/indigenousleaders

Paul says it best, "So let's keep focused on that goal, those of us who want everything God has for us" (Philippians 3:15 MSG).

I pray that God's indescribable joy and abundant blessings flow through your life.

Huni'gum
Siera Taketchera Russell, J.D., M.Ed.
Native American Cross-cultural Consultant & Success Coach

PAY IT FORWARD

I hope my book blessed you.

May I ask you for a quick favor? It means a lot to me.

Please let me know how my message blessed you by sharing your testimony.

It's easy to post your testimony on Amazon and say how my book inspired or encouraged you. Simply write from your heart.

A review not only helps me but also helps others discover these success secrets.

It's amazing how one positive review combines with others and rapidly spreads this message like wildfire.

Please go to: Review.IndigenousMentors.com

I'm excited to read your review as soon as it's available!

Huni'gum

Siera

ACKNOWLEDGMENTS

I want to thank:

- Donna Partow, writing coach, and Tamera Aragon, business coach, for their life-changing Rapid Writing Program and the 7 Days to Freedom Event.

- The Assembly of Believers Prayer Group whose prayer support is priceless.

- Pastor Rob and Vicky Biggs, Pastor Bill and Jan Gowey, and Pastor Larry and Thala Jackson for their love and encouragement to share my message with the world.

- Beta readers and cheerleaders: Debby Brawner, Tim Brown, Honorable Judge Kyle Fields, Becky Hilder, Maureen Kane, Paula Newman, Lura Olander, Pastor David Smith, and Professor Rebecca Tsosie.

- Contributors and cheerleaders in the Indigenous Mentors Facebook group: Diane Norman, Joy Mosley, Kelly Montejo Fink, Linda Hudgins, Myrna Dougherty, Rachel Chavez, Reverend Sharon Gove, and Viola Jackson.

- My next generation, daughter Sacheen and granddaughter Giovanna, for their love and support.

- The resilient women of the Yavapai-Apache Nation for their sacrifices and contribution to our tribe's sovereignty and well-being.

ABOUT THE AUTHOR

*S*iera Taketchera Russell is the CEO and founder of Indigenous Mentors, a Native American consulting, coaching, training, and mentoring platform.

She's passionate about coaching women in academia, business, tribal government, and Native ministry. Siera provides cultural consulting services for tribal governments, corporations, and education institutions.

She earned a Juris Doctorate from UC Berkeley Law, a Master of Arts in Education from Harvard, and a Bachelor of Arts in Elementary Education, *magna cum laude*, from Arizona State University.

Siera serves as an appellate judge for a Southwest Indian community and oversees her family's retail business. She also serves on the Indian Bible College Board of Trustees and the Living Water Foursquare Church council in Arizona.

In 2016, Siera was elected to a three-year term as a legislative member of her tribal nation's council. Before this office, she was an assistant law professor. She taught Property, Criminal Procedure, Topics in Indian Law, and International Human Rights Law.

Siera is a direct descendant of the Wipukepa, a distinct people of the early Yavapai from central Arizona. Her ancestors were indigenous to the Verde Valley, Oak Creek Canyon, and Boynton Canyon in Central Arizona.

She enjoys discovering Arizona parks and wildlife, especially with family and friends.

In 2021, Siera achieved another dream on her vision board—golfing. On Thanksgiving Day 2021, she played her first nine holes and loved it!

For more information or to contact the author, visit www. IndigenousMentors.com

ALSO BY SIERA RUSSELL

For two decades, she lived a daily battle. Would she press on in her pursuit of the pinnacle of success...or surrender to the constant temptation to self-destruct?

This riveting memoir recounts the journey of an indigenous girl from an impoverished reservation in the American Southwest... all the way to Harvard and U.C. Berkeley Law School. Along the way, the demons from her violent, dysfunctional childhood continue to haunt her steps, dragging her again and again into the depths of addiction and destructive relationships.

Can she overcome the stigma of opioid addiction to fulfill her commitment to lead her tribe forward, discovering faith, hope and love along the way?

In this unforgettable, gut-wrenchingly honest book, Siera shares the difficult choices she made, the price she paid and the reason she continues to believe.

Get Your Copy on Amazon.com

Made in the USA
Monee, IL
05 October 2022

15326340R00057